Contents

Introduction

Becoming an entrepreneur is not always an easy process, but this book is here to guide you along your path to professional success. In this series you will learn how to manage others, balance your personal and professional life, be an effective leader, and much more. Rather than allowing yourself to become overwhelmed by the task at hand, you will learn time management, the value of healthy habits, and useful communication skills.

This is Book 1 in a three part series. The following chapters will guide your understanding of a CEO's mindset, management strategies, and the value of creating a positive culture for your business. We encourage you to engage with the following materials at your own pace, and implement them as you see fit in your professional life.

Being a successful entrepreneur is all about making choices, and this three part series allows you to do just that. Please take advantage of all three e-books. Each contains valuable tools that will enable you to set goals, delegate responsibilities, and discover your highest potential. We wish you the best of luck in the journey you are about to embark on!

Chapter 1: Thinking Like A CEO

Here's an entrepreneur's secret to success: The CEO mindset will make you stand out from the crowd. Every aspiring entrepreneur should think like a CEO. The CEO mindset is the #1 trait that every soon-to-be entrepreneur should have before starting a business. If you're considering becoming an entrepreneur, you need to give your current mindset a complete makeover; it's the first thing you should do before taking on the role of entrepreneur.

The CEO mindset is a simple concept to understand, but applying it is another story. Many entrepreneurs and business owners don't succeed in adapting to it. If being a CEO was easy, everyone would be doing it, right?

The CEO mindset consists of several important qualities that every successful entrepreneur has. To adopt this mindset, you need the following:

- A clear vision of what you want to achieve – know exactly what you want
- Know how to prioritize and make decisions
- Know how to focus on the bigger picture rather than the fine details
- Understand how to outsource, and trust others to get tasks done for you and help you to create your vision
- Have the ability to solve problems quickly and stay on track

Here's another way to explain the CEO mindset: A CEO is a type of leader. The CEO of a company is the head, and everyone must follow the CEO's direction. The most important aspect of the CEO mindset is having a vision. Without a clear vision, you won't know where you want to go. If you don't have the end results in mind, you won't succeed in entrepreneurship. If you don't have any direction, how can you lead others?

Top Tips to Become a Successful Entrepreneur and Get the CEO Mindset

Becoming the CEO is a big position to take on, and not everyone can do it. If you're determined to achieve those big dreams that you have, you can acquire CEO qualities and, ultimately, the CEO mindset. Let's go over what it takes to become a successful entrepreneur:

- **Be brave enough to take responsibility for everything associated with your business.** If you make a mistake, own up to it. If your employee makes a mistake that results in bad feedback from a client and several thousand dollars are lost, be accountable for it. You're the person who has to take on everything associated with your business, the good and the bad. Behind closed doors, you can handle your employees your way. In public, you need to be the one to make apologies and amendments. You represent your company, and you're the decision maker.

Unfortunately, many people have trouble being truly accountable. In most cases, it's easier to blame others. If you're serious about becoming an entrepreneur, you need to have a thick skin, modesty, and the courage to take responsibility and maintain your professional image, no matter how bad things get.

- **Know what your time is worth.** This doesn't refer only to your hourly rate or salary. Rather, this also takes into consideration the value that you put on your time. Let's take this scenario as an example: Mark is the CEO of a well-known digital marketing company. He receives about 15-30 new projects every week. Due to his current workload and time constraints, Mark has to evaluate each new project he receives, and takes five minutes at most to determine if the project is worth his time or not. By the end of the week, he has 3-5 new projects he can work on the following week.

When you're the CEO, you don't have time to dawdle. You must make quick decisions for simple situations and get back to more critical parts of your business. That's why it's important for you to know how much your time is worth. Even if you receive a project that's worth thousands of dollars, you have to let it go if there are reasons why you can't accept it, such as a difficult client, other projects that are currently occupying your time, etc.

- **Plan ahead.** Ask any successful CEO or entrepreneur you know whether they plan ahead. Nine out of 10 will say they do. If you want to be successful, you need to plan ahead. If you want to have more time available to you, you need to plan ahead. Know what you want to accomplish during the week. Create to-do lists and set up an organization system for all of your tasks. Planning ahead is a simple habit to get into. Find the best tools that you can use for planning in advance.

Preparing Yourself to Lead

Many people have the misconception that some individuals are born leaders, but that's not the case at all. Qualities and traits of a leader can be acquired, and you can do that by improving yourself. If you're determined to continue on your path to become a successful entrepreneur, you'll need to prepare yourself to become a true leader.

Qualities of a Leader

Certain qualities help to make people into effective leaders or authority figures. Whether the situation at hand is a small group of kids on the playground or a large company, specific traits come into play that make others want to follow leaders. Here's a list of qualities that can help to make you a better leader:

- **Quality #1: Ability to create a vision and make it a reality.** Do you have a clear vision of what you want to achieve and do you believe you can make it a reality? Even if you think the vision is completely out of reach, the main element to focus on here is whether you believe in yourself enough to make that dream become a reality. That's the difference between people who just wish for things they want and people who take steps to make it happen.

- **Quality #2: Risk-taker.** In the business world, you'll never be in the safe zone. You'll be around risks all the time, no matter what decisions you make. To become a true entrepreneur, you must be a risk-taker. You need to move forward and continue on, even if the decision you make is filled with risks. Having the courage to take risks and stop playing it safe will help you to get closer to the finish line.

- **Quality #3: Honesty.** It's simple: Honesty will help you to earn respect and trust, not only with people who work for you, but also with people external to your business such as your customers. Honesty leads to more trusting, loyal relationships, and it also helps build your integrity. You owe it to yourself and to others to always be honest.

This doesn't mean you have to be mean or rude to others. Honesty only means telling the truth. For instance, if you don't agree with someone's work ethics, you can be upfront about this without causing unnecessary trouble.

- **Quality #4: Sharp focus.** To get into the CEO mindset, your eyes should always be on the prize: your vision. Your focus should always be on what you want to accomplish through your business. Your vision creates your path, and that path only leads to one end. That's where your focus needs to be at all times. If anything gets in your way, you need to jump over it and move forward.

Focus isn't limited to your vision, though. As a leader you must focus on other aspects of your business as well, such as the strengths of your employees (rather than their weaknesses.) Not only do you need to have keen focus, you will also need to have the ability to get your workers to focus, too. The followers will mimic their leader. Your people will notice every little thing you do and adopt your behaviors themselves, even if they don't consciously realize this. The more focused you are, the more focused your team will be.

- **Quality #5: Passion.** Do you love what you do? Do you love sharing your passion? Passion is one of the most important qualities found in CEOs and entrepreneurs. Passion is what drives you to achieve your dreams, no matter how out-of-reach they seem to be. The more passionate you are about what you do, the more followers you'll have and the more people you'll be able to call up on to help you to achieve your vision.

- **Quality #6: Persistence.** Entrepreneurs are risk takers. Even if they fail, they continue to move forward and focus on their main goal. Take Colonel Sanders, the founder of KFC, one of the top fast food chains in the U.S. He promoted his chicken to many restaurants across the U.S., but he was rejected every time. In fact, he was rejected over 1,000 times. But he persisted and kept going until he got a "yes." And we all know how that story ended!

  Even if you're not aiming to be a multimillion-dollar business, the point is persistence. Especially when you face difficult obstacles, persistence is one of the secrets to success. The more you want something, the more you'll persist. The more you believe in something, the more you'll persist. No matter how long it takes to reach your dreams, persistence is one of the most important (yet often undervalued) traits that CEOs and entrepreneurs possess.

- **Quality #7: Excellent emotional management.** CEOs are always professional, composed, and calm. They're understanding and empathetic, but they don't let their emotions rule over them. Emotional management is essential to becoming a successful, well-respected entrepreneur.

  Imagine yourself as an A-list celebrity. As a celebrity, you have an image to maintain; if you let emotions get the better of you, you'll most likely see your face on the cover of a celebrity gossip magazine. As the owner of your business, you represent your brand. That's why it's important for you to have complete control over your emotions. Stay composed and calm around others. Show people you have what it takes to be the CEO. Now, this doesn't mean being arrogant and demanding. In fact, another quality that leaders have is humility. Be humble and control your emotions to maintain your image as well as your brand's reputation.

How to Become a Great Leader

You know the *what* when it comes to being a great leader, and now you'll learn the *how*. Below are leadership strategies and advice to help transform you into a great leader:

- **Craft your brand's image.** This doesn't mean the logo, by the way. Your brand's image is an expression of how you want people to perceive your business. Is your brand fun and casual? Is your brand unique and "out there"? Consider how you want to portray your brand.

  How does this relate to being a leader? Your brand's image influences every part of your business, from marketing to business culture. You're the main representative of your brand, and you need to show others (such as your employees) how you want your brand to be seen. That's your role as the leader.

- **Find the silver lining in every bad situation.** No matter how bad a situation is, find the silver lining. True leaders always push forward and stay positive. It may be tempting to curl into a ball, suck your thumb, and cry yourself to sleep, but that's not what a CEO would do. You're a professional, and you're an entrepreneur. You'll move on and overcome any obstacle in your way.

With every problem you face, consider it a challenge instead. The word *problem* has a negative connotation for most people. *Challenge* is easier on the mind, so you'll have a better chance of finding a solution and overcoming a challenge rather than a problem.

Focus on positivity and solutions for every challenge you face. Entrepreneurs are people who find solutions for problems; that's how they start their businesses. They find a problem, and they provide a solution for that problem.

Learn to listen to others. Listening is a skill that every entrepreneur needs. When you share your vision with others, such as your employees, you need to learn to listen to ideas, feedback, etc. You may think your idea is great, but others may not. It's good for you to learn how to listen and understand others.

One useful method to improve your listening skills and foster effective communication with others is to repeat what they say in your own words. This helps you to confirm that you've understood what someone has said, and it also helps the other person to feel they are being listened to.

Be inspirational. You passion is the key to being an inspirational leader. If you have passion and positivity, you'll naturally inspire the people around you. Think about it: If you were negative and disconnected, do you think people would be attracted to you or repelled by your attitude? Repelled, of course. Positivity and passion are the basics of an inspirational leader.

Inspirational leaders also help to motivate their people to take action and become a meaningful part of the business. Rewards, recognition, and regular praise are great ways to motivate your team members.

- **Be open to trying new things.** Even though you're the leader, you won't always have the best ideas or the best approaches. For example, if you have an idea for a marketing campaign but a marketing expert on your team says it won't do well and offers an alternative idea, try it.

Just because you're the boss, this doesn't mean you're the expert in every area of your business.

CEOs are people who create visions, and they delegate tasks to skillful people to make those visions a reality. CEOs don't have to know everything in detail about the various areas of their businesses. That's why it's important for leaders to be open and try new things. You may be pleasantly surprised in the end.

A major tip for becoming a great leader is to be your own leader. Be a leader that effectively converys who you are and fits with how you want to represent your brand. Create your own definition of an effective leader and follow it. Remember to include the basic traits of a leader in your definition as well.

CEOs Make Sacrifices

Sacrifices are part of the entrepreneurial world, and some of the sacrifices you'll have to make will be difficult. Sacrifices are made based on what you value the most. This is also based on how you manage your tasks and your overall schedule. For instance, if you put off certain business tasks for another day that happens to coincide with a family event, you will have to choose one or the other. As part of your entrepreneurial journey, you must accept the fact that you'll have to make sacrifices. You will also need to make difficult decisions, and there will be times when all of your options will not be favorable.

One of the most common sacrifices that CEOs make is related to the balance between their work and home lives. For example, some CEOs may work 60 hours per week or more because they put their business first, while other CEOs work only 20-30 hours per week and spend most of their time with their families. One spends less time with family while the other spends less time in their businesses.

There's no right or wrong choice when it comes to making sacrifices or deciding where to spend your time. You will need to make the decision that is right for you. In some cases, the sacrifices you make can help you to realize what you value most in life and how you want to prioritize your responsibilities. With this in mind, you'll be able to make better choices in the future when you're faced with a situation where you must choose one thing over another.

If you think you'll have trouble maintaining your work-life balance while you pursue your business goals, here's a list of great tips that you can apply to your life:

- **Identify boundaries and stick with them.** If you want to make sure you spend tons of time with your family after work, determine what time you'll leave the office and go back home, such as at 5 p.m. every weekday. Once you've decided on a time, cut off all connections to your work, such as your laptop or work phone, once that time rolls around each day. Avoid letting yourself slip. Stick with your boundaries at all times, and make no exceptions. If you do let things slide, you'll be prone to letting even more things slide and may end up with an unhealthy work-life balance.

- **Wake up earlier.** If you want to get more work-related tasks completed, wake up earlier. Alternatively, you can also spend the mornings with your family and spend the rest of your day at work. Make time for what you want to accomplish during your day. Waking up earlier will help you do just that.

- **Delegate tasks.** If you have simple yet time-consuming tasks on your to-do list, outsource them. Focus on the bigger, more important tasks on your list and cross them off one by one while other people help you to complete the rest of your tasks. Just like a true CEO, outsourcing tasks will help you to accomplish your goals more quickly.

- **Know when to say "no."** CEOs know when to say "no," so make sure you learn to do that, too. If you take on too much and become a "yes" man or woman, you'll stress yourself out and become just another employee in your business. You're the boss, so you can say "yes" or "no" to anything you want. If you are presented with a new project that someone proposed to you but you're swamped already, you can kindly reject the offer and continue working on other tasks. You won't run out of projects to work on, so you don't need to worry about that. Don't focus on scarcity. Remember, you're the CEO. You need to focus on the bigger picture. If rejecting a project will help you in the long run, do it.

Prepare to Lose it All

While we're on the topic of making sacrifices, let's talk about the possibility of losing your entire business. Keep in mind that this is just a slim possibility, but every aspiring entrepreneur should consider this possibility and prepare for it.

Preparing for disaster doesn't mean it's going to happen. It just means you have a plan in place in case a disaster does occur.

Even with all the hard work that's put into building a business, sometimes it doesn't work out. The business ends up failing and crumbling to the ground. Some of the common reasons that businesses fail include:

- Financial trouble, such as not being able to meet payroll, not having a steady cash flow, and not keeping track of payments
- Wasting time and money on a bad business idea
- Not having a good pricing plan in place
- Working too much *in* your business instead of *on* your business, which leads to burnouts and a loss of passion
- Poor marketing strategies
- Failing to evaluate competitors regularly
- Unhappy employees and customers

A lot of the reasons why businesses fail can be fixed, but business owners often fail to realize that they have a problem until it's too late. When your business isn't doing as well as you initially thought it would, that doesn't mean you've already given up the opportunity to find the leak, fix it right away, and watch your business come back to life. Here are some signs to look out for if you think your business is going downhill:

- You don't have a steady cash flow to pay those business expenses.
- You're not promoting your products or services to the right market, so you're receiving low sales or no sales at all.
- Your brand looks like every other brand out there.
- You're not managing your business finances properly.
- Your employees aren't making progress in their assignments.
- You're not focused on your business and aren't spending enough time on it.
- You lack passion for your business and you're only after the money.

- You're guessing at what to do with your business rather than knowing exactly what you want to do, or you don't have a clear vision.
- You have poor business management skills.
- You don't have the CEO mindset.

If you notice any of these signs in yourself, stop what you're doing and evaluate your entire business. Write down any challenges you face, and figure out solutions to them. Ask yourself: How can I overcome this challenge? Brainstorm ideas for solutions, and see if you can get your business back on top.

If your business is already in too deep, you should cut back on costs immediately. You can also liquidate your assets if you need fast cash. Your assets may include office furniture, electronics and equipment.

At this point, you can call it quits and walk away from the entrepreneurial world for a while and come back later on when you have a better grasp of business management. You can also find a mentor or consultant to help you sort out your business and see if you can get it up and running again.

True failure happens only when you give up, and stop growing and improving. If you let a business failure stop you from achieving your dreams, that's the truest form of failure. Businesses can be built again, so don't let yourself get too down about a business failure. If you can save your business, even if it's hanging by a thread, do it as long as you still have a passion for it.

Making Your Dreams Come True
No one wants their business to fail. If you believe in your business idea wholeheartedly and you're honest with yourself, you can make your dreams become realities.

When it comes to making your dreams come true, what you need the most are the three Ps: persistence, patience, and positivity. Entrepreneurs make mistakes and may fail lots of times before they achieve success. They reach their goals because they are persistent. They continue onwards despite their failures. Even if you feel uncomfortable or paralyzed with fear, continue moving forward.

Patience is another important trait to have because you can't put a time limit on your dreams if you want to achieve them. Your dreams will manifest on their own time as long as you persist and work on them regularly.

As for positivity, positive thoughts will lead you to your dreams faster. If you only think negatively or worry about your dreams, you'll unintentionally prevent yourself from achieving them. Let go of your fears and worries because they're all in your head. If you want to be an entrepreneur, the three Ps are essential ingredients for your success.

Another important note about reaching your goals: Accept that you'll have to make changes to make your business work. You may have already created a detailed business plan, but this doesn't mean your business will go according to plan. Be open to changes because you most likely will have to make many changes to your business on the path to success. You're not focusing on the *how* of accomplishing your goals, you're focusing on the *end result*. The *how* doesn't matter if you concentrate on getting to the finish line instead.

CEOs Tell it Like it Is

This section emphasizes a trait that every CEO needs: assertiveness. As was mentioned before, to have the CEO mindset, you need to know what you want. On top of that, you need to know how to get what you want and put effort into working toward your goal every day. When you know what you want, you'll make better decisions and you'll have an easier time trimming the fat from your business by prioritizing and outsourcing tasks.

Being assertive means you always stand up for your beliefs, your vision, and your business. You already know what you want. If anyone or anything becomes an obstacle in your way, your assertiveness will help you to overcome it. For example, let's say there's another entrepreneur who wants to partner with you on a project, but he doesn't share the same work ethics as you do and you end up disagreeing over many aspects of the work. When you realize that the partnership isn't going to be successful, you nip it in the bud and let the other party know it's not going to work for you.

As an entrepreneur, the ability to stand by your values, your beliefs, your vision, etc. is vital. If you hesitate when making decisions or try to please others because you want to look good and save face, you'll end up in more trouble than is truly necessary. That's why it's important to know what you want and to be assertive. If you waver with every decision and don't stick to your work ethics, your journey toward becoming a successful entrepreneur won't be an easy one.

The Right Way to Fire People

Along with being assertive toward people outside your business, you also need to be assertive with the people working for you. Once again, you need to know what you want and communicate your expectations to the people in your business.

When an employee isn't helping your business to grow and is only hindering progress, it may be time to let the person go. Assertiveness comes into play here as well because you need to think of the bigger picture. Remind yourself of what you want to achieve in your business. Remind yourself of your vision. Now, ask yourself this: Would you let one employee stop you from achieving the big prize at the end?

This is not to say it's alright to treat people like dirty rags and toss them out when you don't need them anymore. Think of your business this way: You're basically trading money and other benefits for other people's time and skill. However, if someone isn't performing well and isn't bringing you the results you want, you can let them go. The problem employee isn't keeping up his or her end of the bargain, so you don't need to continue the relationship anymore.

When it's time to fire workers, there's a right way to do it. Ideally, you should do the firing instead of relying on someone else to do it. This is because you'll know exactly what went down during the conversation instead of hearing it from another person. Another reason to do it yourself is because you'll gain more respect and credibility. Although firing people isn't pleasant, your employees will have a better understanding of why you're letting them go. Firing people yourself will also help to seal the deal, so to speak, and provide closure for everyone.

To fire people the right way –not the Donald Trump way – here's a step-by-step guide:

1. Make sure you're doing it for the right reasons. Countless reasons are used for firing people, but some of them aren't fair or honest. For the sake of your integrity, make sure you fire people for the right reasons. If an employee doesn't fit with your business culture and makes everyone else feel out of place, it's most likely time to let him or her go. If an employee isn't helping you to reach the vision you have for your business, you're better off firing the person.

When you're considering firing someone, always think of the bigger picture. That's your job as the leader of your business. You need to look at the big picture and see if something or someone is preventing you from reaching your goals. If so, address this immediately and move on. You're the CEO, and you don't have time to sweep things under the rug or slow down your progress.

In some cases, you can still give people second chances. If an employee made a mistake and you think he or she can bounce back without making the same mistake again, give them another chance. Hiring and firing take a lot of time, especially if you're doing it yourself. You may be pleasantly surprised that an employee, despite making a mistake, can become one of your most valuable workers. However, if you still see the same mistakes being made after talking to the employee about it, it's time to trim the fat and let the employee go for good.

2. Have a firing strategy and prepare all necessary paperwork and other materials.

Before letting anyone go, make sure you have a strategy in place. Know how you're going to start the conversation, and know how you're going to address the issue.

It's best to get straight to the point. Let the employee know he or she hasn't been performing well or meeting your expectations. Let the employee know that you've thought it through and given them multiple chances, but you've decided to let him or her go. Once you've announced this, let the other person talk and take in the information that they're giving you. Give him or her time to process what you've just said. Be empathetic, but don't let your emotions come into the conversation. Remember, your relationship with your employee is all business – nothing personal.

If the employee asks you questions, calmly answer them and maintain your professional image. If the employee gets upset or angry and starts to behave negatively, ask him or her to calm down and ask if he or she needs a moment alone. Leave the room for a few minutes if the person needs you to. During this entire experience, make sure your emotions don't sway you. As the boss, you can't let other people's actions influence your decisions or emotions. You must stand firm in what you believe in, even if other people think you're in the wrong.

When you're firing someone, you should have someone else with you to witness the situation. This is to protect yourself in case the employee tries to turn the event into a legal matter. Also, if the employee threatens you or becomes violent, having a witness present may help your case.

Once everything has been said and done, give the individual all of the necessary information and paperwork he or she needs to complete the firing process.

3. Wrap up the firing procedure and move on. You've finally pushed through the hard part. It's time to move on and continue working toward your vision. If you need another worker, you can start searching for one at this stage.

Firing people can be nerve-wracking, but being prepared can help you to feel less nervous and stand firm in your decision. You should also remember to put your CEO cap on when you're firing people. When you think like a CEO, you'll have an easier time letting employees go. The CEO mindset is powerful and will help you to stick to your decisions.

Chapter 2: The Three Ps – People, Products and Processes

Starting and managing a business as the owner is on a completely different playing field from what you're probably used to. You have multiple areas to manage and focus on, mainly the people, the products, and the processes or procedures involved. "The people" represents those who work for you. "The products" are what you offer to the public. "The processes or procedures" are how you organize different areas of your business and manage the flow of each area.

The People

Part One: Building a Positive Workplace

Creating a positive workplace for yourself and your team is an essential part of your job as the business owner. Even a drop of negativity can strain the team's overall performance. That's why positivity should be at the foundation of your work environment.

Positivity does more than put smiles on people's faces and create a friendly atmosphere. Positivity helps you and your employees to increase productivity, make better decisions, brainstorm more effectively, and much more. A positive workplace will enable you to get positive results. Here are some fantastic tips on how to do just that:

1. **Provide training materials that encourage your future employees to take on a positive attitude.** If people want to work in your business, they'll adapt to the positive attitude required to be a part of your team. Remember, you're the leader and this is your business. You want it to be a certain way, so you have to enforce the positive outlook that's required yourself in order to build a positive workplace. You make the rules here; don't be afraid to command that people have a positive mindset when they work for you.

One of the ways to prep future employees for your positive work environment is to incorporate what you expect in your training materials. Before anyone enters your business and becomes a part of it, you must express your expectations. This helps you to pick out the bad eggs and narrow down your list of potential hires to employees who will adapt to a positive business setting.

No matter what position people are applying for, every piece of training material you provide should start by introducing what you expect from your workers. Let them learn about your business and your expectations right from the start; this makes it easier for new workers to transition into your workplace.

2. Focus on people's strengths. Building confidence among your employees is another important part of being the CEO. The more confidence someone has, the better results he or she will produce.

If you give a written project to someone who isn't skilled at writing, what will you get in return? Amateur results, of course, and those results can affect your business negatively. The person who is working on the assignment would feel inadequate about his or her skills as well, resulting in even more half-hearted outcomes.

When you focus on people's strengths and assign projects according to people's skill sets you'll get the best results, and ultimately this will help to grow your business. Also, by focusing on each person's strengths, you give your workers a reason to enjoy their work and encourage them to help you grow and improve your business. In exchange for optimal results, when you focus on each person's strengths you get happier employees.

Avoid assigning tasks and projects to people who won't excel at them. Make sure you consider who the best person is for each task before you delegate; otherwise, you won't get the results you want.

3. Be open and respectful toward your people. You may be the boss, but that doesn't mean you should stop respecting the people in your workplace.

During meetings and brainstorming sessions with your team, be open-minded and consider everyone's ideas. Make everyone feel like they're an important part of your business. Learn to listen to others.

The golden rule – treat others how you want to be treated – plays a major role in creating a positive work environment. You're the leader, and your employees are your followers. They will follow your example, and they will do what you require them to do. If you don't respect your people, they won't respect you.

This is why it's incredibly important to consider everyone's ideas, thoughts, and feelings, and treat them in the most appropriate way. If someone's ideas don't work for your business or vision, you don't have to approve of them; but you should still provide feedback and explain why certain ideas won't work. Don't dismiss them and move on without providing feedback.

4. Give credit where credit is due. If your team members have contributed greatly to projects and your overall business, give them the praise they deserve. Even small wins deserve a pat on the back and recognition from the boss. Remember, your employees aren't just people who are doing work for you; they're helping your business in many ways.

To help boost the positive attitude among your team members, give praise regularly. You don't have to do it every day, but even a small "thank you" goes a long way. If a worker did something small and unrelated to work assignments, such as getting more paper towels for the restrooms, remember to express your gratitude.

Praise and gratitude are two of the most effective ways to build a positive workplace. They're also contagious. Over time, you'll notice your employees treating each other with respect, expressing gratitude, and even praising each other for a job well done. Keep an eye on your employees and the fantastic work they do, and continue to praise and encourage them.

5. Provide weekly or monthly employee evaluations. Let workers know how they're contributing to the business and how they're progressing with weekly or monthly evaluations. Evaluations are effective because they help employees to know how they're helping your business grow. They also help employees to know which areas need improvement. Evaluations can also be used to provide employees with feedback on projects they've completed.

To start giving evaluations, organize task lists and identify the goals associated with each employee. You can do this at the beginning of each week or month, depending on your business and nature of the work assignments. Once you've figured out the goals that you want each worker to achieve, determine how you want to track their progress. You can ask your employees to keep an activity log and send it to you at the end of each day. At the end of the week or month, you can provide more accurate evaluations of each employee based onteh reports as well as the work you have received, and provide more specific feedback.

Performing regular evaluations instead of annual ones is more effective because they encourage employees to continue improving themselves throughout the year. Your business can change at any time and your team needs to be able to adjust to the changes as they come. If you wait until the end of the year to provide evaluations, you'll delay progress and business growth that you could be making sooner.

Schedule regular evaluations and follow this schedule to ensure that you stay on top of employee progress.

6. Hire positive people from the start. To reduce the risk of hiring people who won't help you to build a positive workplace, hire positive people from the start. The hiring process can be tedious and you may think, "I just want to get this over with!" but you'll save more time in the long run by hiring the right people for your business.

You may read through many impressive resumes, but the individuals themselves may have personalities and attitudes that don't fit with what you want in your employees. In some cases, you may discover great people who don't have extensive experience or skills. If you come across these types of people, see if they're willing to learn and improve themselves while they work for you. That's the important part. Everyone should have a chance to improve themselves, so you may start out hiring an average worker but end up cultivating a fantastic employee who beats the rest.

The only time when you may not need to focus as much on personality and attitude is if you hire online freelancers. If you're the only person from your business who communicates with these employees, you can be more lenient about your business environment.

Be careful, though – your leniency may overflow into your offline business and affect your mindset in your physical workplace. Create a thick, bold boundary line between virtual workers and employees in the physical office. If you and your team work with freelancers directly, you should work with independent contractors who fit into your business culture.

7. Set up at least one area in your office where employees can take a break from work. Give your employees a break from the work routine and set up an area for them to relax and have fun. In-office gyms or lounges make excellent break rooms for your workers. Designating an area for your employees to remove themselves from the work environment will help them to relax and refresh their minds before going back to work. It'll also help to increase productivity.

You can also go the extra mile and provide refreshments and even weekly lunches for your team. Treat them to healthy snacks and beverages so they can maintain their energy levels and continue working on assignments effectively throughout the day.

Here's a bonus tip to help you create a more supportive and positive workplace for yourself and your employees: Give your employees schedule flexibility. Work-life balance can be challenging for most people. If you provide flexibility that allows your employees to do their work at home and schedule their work around their personal lives, it'll be more favorable for both you and your workers. Just remember to use an effective system and make sure everyone completes their work on time.

The People
Part Two: Developing a Business Culture

Yes, you can develop your own culture, even in business. No matter the size of your business, you can create a fantastic culture that represents your brand, gives your business direction, and helps your team members give life to your business culture.

Your business culture can be anything you want it to be. Your business culture is based around your business values, vision, goals, practices, and brand. Your business culture signifies not only your business brand, but also how you direct your employees. Your work environment is also determined by how you want to develop your business culture. Here's a step-by-step guide to build the foundation for your business culture and nurture it:

1. Start with your vision. The vision you had before you started your business should be the first piece of your business culture. Your vision is the center of your business. Everything you do is aimed towards achieving that vision, from hiring the right people to creating smaller goals and strategies. Make sure you know exactly what your vision is. Write it down in detail if this will help you.

2. Figure out your business values. Business values vary from CEO to CEO. If you need help figuring out your business values, ask yourself these questions:

- What do I value most in my business?
- How do I want to present my company to the public?
- What type of people do I want to work with? (e.g. creative, funny, positive, etc.)
- How do I want to set up my business? (e.g. have schedule flexibility, don't work on weekends, no overtime, etc.)
- What is my vision and what values are needed to accomplish my vision?

- How far am I willing to go to achieve my main objectives?

Create a list of possible values to work from. Research the values of other companies, or even your competitors, to see if you can get inspiration from their values.

You don't have to figure out all of your business values at the beginning. Values change over time in businesses, especially when you develop relationships with other people such as your employees and customers. Start with a handful of values and add to or change them as necessary. If you already have partners and employees whom you trust before you launch your business, you can discuss values and choose the best ones to use to develop a business culture that fits your image.

3. Hire the right people. Building a positive workplace and developing a great business culture requires hiring the right people. Focus on hiring to build your culture first, before you get enticed by someone's resume. Think about whether you'll get along with the person before you invite him or her into your business.

4. Match the way you manage your business with modern lifestyles. Society is always changing and the way you manage your business should follow these changes. Technology is one example of how you can improve the way you organize and manage your business to match modern lifestyles. Don't get stuck in another era when it comes to developing your business culture. Connect your business to today's world. Change the way you handle your business and upgrade when necessary.

5. Focus on building a culture where your team members don't need you to keep the business going. If something happens to you or if you want to take a long vacation from your business, can you trust your employees to make the right decisions in your abscence? Can you trust your employees to get things done without you being there?

The best business culture is one where you're not needed. This doesn't mean you'll lose your position as the owner or CEO. When you create a culture where you can trust people to carry on the work without you being there, it means you've achieved the ultimate business culture. You have employees that you can trust enough to basically think the way you do and make decisions based on that understanding. Even without you there, your business continues to grow.

To help you develop such a culture, we're going back to important advice that has already been mentioned: Hire the right people. You should hire people whom you know will invest their time in their jobs wholeheartedly. Choose people whom you know can make good decisions that will benefit your business. Hire individuals whom you can consider partial owners of the business. If you can't trust your employees or let them manage their projects on their own, you're not ready to become a CEO.

No matter how you define your business culture, make sure you do three things as soon as you've figured out the culture you want to develop: Teach your culture, live your culture, and adapt your culture.

When you're recruiting, you have to teach your culture to prepare your new employees. You're the leader of your business. If you don't live your culture when you're at work – or even in your personal life – how can your workers follow you? If you believe in your culture, live it. Last but not least, change your culture when necessary. Businesses change all the time, and a business's culture can change as well. If you see that your business culture needs to be adapted, adjusted or changed in some way to make it better, do it. Avoid delaying the change.

The People
Part Three: Why You Need to Train Your Employees
Part of both building a positive work environment and developing a superb business culture is to start

with your employees. Many business owners avoid training their employees properly due to the time and monetary investment that goes into training. Training employees adequately has many benefits, including better performance, meeting expectations and goals, better product quality, and encouraging them to stay in your business for a long time. Training also helps workers to prepare for successful participation in your business, which means less time wasted and fewer mistakes made.

You should do the training yourself or have someone else who's very familiar with your business do the training. Many businesses outsource training to other companies, but this method isn't as effective as in-house training. Outside companies don't understand your business like you do. Creating your own training materials and providing the training yourself will build a better business culture and help your employees to understand your business more.

Before you start training anyone, make a list of the areas in your business that need employee training.

Consider your goals and which job positions you need to fill to achieve those goals. In some job positions, extensive training isn't necessary; a basic guide will do. Make sure you go over the basics of your business with every employee, such as business values, your target market, vision, culture, work attire, etc.

The next task you should do is determining the best way to train your employees. Many people learn better with visual aids, such as training videos. You can also schedule personal training sessions with employees and give them one-on-one training. Here are some suggestions for creating your training materials:

- Slideshows
- Videos
- Seminars
- Workshops
- Illustrated training guides
- Podcasts with accompanying e-books
- Using real-life scenarios as part of the training

process
- Personal one-on-one training

If possible, make your training materials and activities fun and exciting. Add humorous and creative elements to your training. Even if you're training your employees personally, you can still make it fun and personal.

Once you get training out of the way, you should keep track of your employees' progress and prepare additional, more fine-tuned or detailed training materials in case you need to provide additional or more extensive training. Set up a progress-tracking system, such as a practice of providing weekly evaluations, to help you keep track of your employees' progress.

As your business changes over time, prepare training videos and update training materials to help employees adjust to these changes. For example, if some workers will have to take on more tasks, you should prepare them ahead of time and provide them with the necessary training.

Another aspect of training to consider is whether the materials truly help your employees. At the end of training sessions, you can do a survey of your team members and get feedback from them to help improve their training. By getting feedback from others, you'll learn whether your training materials are effective. Then you can improve future employee training sessions and get better results.

Preparing employee training resources takes a lot of time and perhaps even money, depending on the methods you use. Think of this as a major investment in your business. Not only does training employees give you better results and help to grow your business, you may also build your ideal business environment through effective training. You don't have to spend a fortune on employee training, especially if you're just starting out. You'll have better workers and a better overall business culture when you properly train your employees.

The People

Part Four: Why Employees Misinterpret Managers – And How to Fix This

Employees and managers don't always have the friendliest of relationships. Since their positions are different, misunderstandings can occur. Think of the manager-employee relationship as something similar to the parent-child relationship.

The manager is doing his or her job to ensure that employees are meeting deadlines, making progress, and helping the business grow overall. The manager focuses on the bigger picture and aims to improve the working environment. Employees are like the puzzle pieces that combine to form the bigger picture. They focus on smaller tasks and are responsible for meeting deadlines and the expectations of their superiors. Most workers don't see the bigger picture like the manager does. It's the same thing as a parent with his or her child. The child is focused on the smaller details of life, such as playing and simply living in the moment. The parent is focused on the bigger picture – the child's future and how the child's decisions and behavior can affect his or her future.

The parent's view is similar to the manager's view: he or she focuses on the future while the child and the employee often focus on the present. This isn't to say that employees are childish or that they should be treated like children. Rather, this is just a simple analogy to help you understand why employees can sometimes misunderstand managers. One of the reasons employees misinterpret managers is because they don't share the manager's position and mindset, which is illustrated in the parent-child relationship analogy.

Another reason employees often misunderstand managers is because of their own mindsets. For example, if an employee receives criticism of his or her work, he or she may adopt the victim mindset and wonder, "Why am I the only one being criticized?" The reality is that the manager does critique other employees, and the manager is doing this only to improve results as well as the workplace environment. There are many ways for employees to misunderstand their manager's actions, so what can you do to ensure that there's a civil relationship between your workers and managers? Let's go over a few helpful tips to do just that:

1. Be transparent about people's positions and roles in the business. Some employees may not know what their manager actually does while he or she is at work. To create a more open relationship between your managers and employees, be transparent about each person's role in the company. For instance, in training materials you can describe various people's roles and explain what's expected of them so that employees may understand each other's positions.

2. Train your managers to handle problems quickly and maintain clear, open lines of communication. Your managers are there to maintain a positive, productive workplace. If problems arise, it's the manager's job to handle them effectively. Your training should include the best ways to address common issues that may come up at work.

Tell managers how you want them to handle problems that affect the workplace, but let employees sort out personal problems among themselves. Managers aren't parents, so they don't have to address every little problem. Employees should be able to maintain civil relationships among themselves.

Instead of letting your managers deal with every small issue that comes their way, tell them to encourage employees to work it out themselves. Managers can guide employees to resolutions; they don't have to necessarily fix every problem. Most people don't enjoy confrontation, so a little guidance can help ease people into solving their own problems at work.

3. Hire people who have good judgment. Being objective is an important trait for managers to have, especially when it comes to dealing with complicated situations at work. By being objective, you will have better judgment and can determine the best way to handle a dilemma. Right from the start, hire people who have good judgment and who are able to remain calm and composed during tough times.

To determine if someone has good judgment, you can ask him or her scenario-based questions to determine how they would handle hypothetical problems. Their answers will tell you who may be the best manager for your team.

Another important quality that a manager should possess is that of a team player. Hire managers who value teamwork, can help build employee relationships, and foster cooperation.

4. Make sure your managers do what they say. Actions speak louder than words, after all. People notice and remember actions more than words, so make sure your managers are doing their work properly. Your managers are the leaders of your employee team, in the same way that you're the leader of your business. They should practice what they preach.

Your managers should have leadership qualities to help them perform better at their jobs. Managers should always be consistent with their words and actions. Do weekly or monthly evaluations of your managers and ask your employees how they're doing while working under your managers. This will give you insight as to how your managers are doing and if they need constructive criticism of their performance.

5. Help employees find common ground with each other. One of the best ways to help employees to get along is to have them interact with each other often and find common ground among themselves. For example, three of your employees have dogs but five have cats. Even if there's a friendly rivalry between dog and cat lovers, they have a common interest: animals. You can set up regular events and outings, such as weekend picnics, to keep a positive work environment.

The People

Part Five: Bringing Big Company Executives into Small Businesses

Big company executives have fantastic resumes and skill sets. Their experience and knowledge can help your business grow. The potential problem here doesn't lie in their experience and job history – it's in their ability to adapt to a small business.

Big company executives are used to managing hundreds or even thousands of employees. They're used to people demanding their attention left and right. With small companies, fewer people require management and less attention is needed.

Big company executives may be a mismatch for your business. They may take longer to adjust to your business culture and the way you manage your business. Even if they have tons of experience and knowledge, big company executives will have to completely change their mindsets and working habits to adjust to yours.

This can cause friction among your employees and within your business overall. The big company executives that you want to bring into your small business may be too big for you to handle. For instance, they may have big ideas that won't work for your business. They may not be used to more personal contact with you and other employees, which can cause problems later on and may strain employee relations.

If you want to hire someone who has worked for a big company, consider the risks involved. Remember to hire those who are a good fit with your business culture first. If bringing in a big company executive will ruin the culture of your business, it's best to let the person go.

The Products
The Importance of Quality Assurance

Now that we've wrapped up the people part of the 3 Ps, let's go over the next P: the products. When it comes to offering products or services, quality is the number one element that you should put the most focus on. You don't want your customers to be unsatisfied with your products or services and receive bad feedback, right? If this happens, your company won't build a good reputation. Bad reviews often mean people are likely to be repelled by your business rather than being intrigued by what you're offering.

One of the most popular methods for quality assurance is the Six Sigma approach. Six Sigma helps organizations to measure the quality of the products or services they're offering. This approach has two different ways of measuring quality: the DMAIC process and the DMADV process. Here's the breakdown of each process:

DMAIC		**DMAI**
D	Define	D
M	Measure	M
A	Analyze	A
I	Improve	D
C	Control	V

Depending on your business and what you're offering, you can use one or both processes. You can even use these processes to evaluate other procedures in your business. Learn more about the Six Sigma processes and what they mean here.

The Process

How to Manage Business Debt

It happens all the time: You have more business expenses than you can handle, and you've acquired debt because of them. Debt can cause businesses to crash and go under. This can be a terrifying experience for any business owner. To discuss the last P of the 3 Ps – the processes or procedures – let's go over how to manage business debt, one of the most important management systems you'll need in your business.

1. Evaluate your costs. Many business owners tend to rack up business costs when they don't need to. This is happens for various reasons, such as wanting to look professional. But this is your business, so you don't have to look just like other businesses and drain your wallet in the process. Figure out which business expenses you truly need, such as machinery, office space, etc. Then figure out where you can cut costs and save cash.

2. Create a budget for all expenses. Gain better control over your business finances by creating a budget for all expenses. Put together a budget for the mandatory expenses, such as utilities and salaries. Then create a budget for any other possible expenses you may have, such as new machinery and technology. You never know when you may need to invest in the future of your business.

Save a portion of your revenue for those unexpected purchases. You can also create a business fund for these types of investments and tap into the fund when you need to, just remember to continue putting money into the fund each month.

3. Set up a debt payment system. Dave Ramsey's debt snowball plan is an effective way to prioritize debts and pay them off faster. You may choose to focus on paying off debts that will cost you more later on, such as risking your assets to debt collectors.

4. Find ways to increase your profits. Earning more money can help you to manage and reduce debts. Evaluate your business and see where you can offer more products or services to your current customers and prospects. For example, you can create an e-book that will help your target market and create a passive income stream.

Another way to increase profits is to improve your current marketing campaigns. You may not have to spend anything to make your marketing campaigns better and reel in more customers. If you're on a tight budget, you'll have to be creative about how you increase your profits. This may mean you'll have to do most of the work yourself to lower costs. You can also sell your assets for quick cash if you don't need them for your business.

5. Avoid borrowing money if possible. Loans and credit are considered the easy way out when it comes to managing debt and paying off business expenses. In the end, you're only creating more debt for yourself. If you're considering borrowing money, make sure you can pay it back quickly; you'll pile on the interest if you pay your debts off slowly. Use loans as a last resort solution instead.

The number one tip when it comes to managing your business debt and finances is to review financial statements at the end of each month. Set a day to review all of your financial statements to ensure that you're keeping on top of them. Don't let yourself slip on these reviews, or you may end up with many unpleasant surprises waiting at your door.

Always have a financial management plan in place, even if you decide to delegate financial management to an accountant. Although you may not be an expert with finances, know what's going on with your business moneywise at all times to avoid making mistakes that can cause your business to crash overnight.

Chapter 3: Creating a Positive Business Culture

The inside of your business is just as important as the outside – if not more. Your brand's public image can be affected by what goes on *inside* your business. That's why developing a business culture is crucial. What you do on the inside will show on the outside.

Your business culture is one of the main factors that define your business. From the way you treat your employees to the way you organize the various areas of your business, developing a business culture will provide a guide for how you want to present your business to customers and employees.

The Basics of a Business Culture

Step out of your CEO shoes for a moment and imagine yourself looking for a job. What would be the ideal work environment for you? Now, slip back into your CEO shoes and ask yourself the same question, plus this additional one: Would you still want to be in the same environment, or would you want to change it?

Thinking from the employees' point of view can guide you in developing the right culture for your business. Since you're seeing everything from the employees' point of view, you can imagine what type of work environment you would want to be in, what type of employer you would want to work for, etc. You can also draw from your own experience and knowledge about work environments and use this information to help you figure out the ideal culture for your business.

Also, remember that your vision is the foundation of your business culture. Know what your vision is and let that guide you towards creating the right business environment. To help you figure out the best business setting for you and your employees, consider the following elements:

- **Companionship and Teamwork –**

How do you plan to build strong teamwork among your employees? What events would you like to hold to help your employees create better relationships with each other? (For example, weekend picnics, Friday night outings, etc.)

How will you have fun with your employees and create a sense of camaraderie? Traditions unique to your business can help to build strong connections and teamwork. Your team will always have something to look forward to while working for you.

What occasions do you want to celebrate with your employees? Birthdays and holidays are popular occasions to celebrate. Think about the different ways you can make your business fun and exciting. Business doesn't have to be all about work.

- **Community** – Business owners and their employees help their local communities all the time. Consider whether you'd like your business to be involved in your community. Not only does this help to build better teamwork and camaraderie, it also helps your employees to feel great about the work they do. They'll find personal satisfaction from being involved with your business, thus increasing your chances of retaining them.

- **Communication** – How are you going to communicate with your team members, and how can you help them communicate with each other effectively? Be open to using multiple communication methods. Depending on your business, you may need to employ various methods in order to make better connections with your people.

For example, you can utilize a task management tool that allows you to invite team members to participate. This will provide a way to keep them updated on projects and tasks. You can also create a forum for your team and allow members to post questions anonymously. This helps to eliminate any anxiety or pressure that employees may feel about asking questions in front of others, i.e. during meetings.

Remember to show your employees you care. Even if you're managing hundreds of workers, find a way to be aware of what's going on in their lives. You can set up a form that employees can fill out when big events happen in their lives, such as weddings, births, and deaths. Once you receive these messages, you can send the individuals personal notes, gifts, etc. to show you care.

- **Core Values** – Core values are the beliefs your business holds. Every person in the business should follow these core values. These values determine the way you organize your business, the decisions you make, and much more. For example, if you value culture more than having employees with amazing resumes, one of your values can be something like, "All employees need to be team players."

- **Organization** – From procedures to schedules, your business needs an organizational system. If you don't follow an organizational system, it'll only cause stress and chaos for you and your employees. You'll most likely use more than one organizational system for different areas of your business. Pick the best one for each area of your business.

- **Training** – A major part of your business culture is the training you provide to current and future employees. There's a difference between a company that has a training program for employees to continually improve themselves and a company that doesn't invest in training at all.

  Determine the most appropriate approach for training. It's best if you provide the training materials yourself instead of outsourcing this task to another company. You know your business the best, and it's vital for your team to know your business as closely as you do. Otherwise, they may not produce the results you want.

  One way to provide effective training for your employees is to develop a learning center in your office, or even online. You can provide resources to help employees improve themselves or to update team members of any new developments in your business.

- **Strong Leadership** – You're the head of your team, and your leadership skills need to be strong and influential. You control what goes on in your business, and you must be consistent with your decisions. You can make changes as time goes by, but a leader who constantly makes changes and is indecisive can't be an effective leader. Determine what type of leader you are and what values and skills you need in order to be the leader you want to be.

These are the general elements that are incorporated in most business cultures, but they're not mandatory. You can create any type of business culture you want.

Devise a model that works for you and your business. Managing a business is different than managing your personal life. With more at stake and more people to oversee, you need to be firm about business management. Focus on your business culture. Nurture a positive work environment that boosts your business instead of dragging it down.

How to Minimize Politics Within the Company

No, we're not talking about government politics here. Company politics is another playing field, and it can be one of the most frustrating aspects of working in a company. Even if the CEO makes it clear that he or she doesn't play the company politics game, somehow it develops nonetheless and becomes part of the work environment.

Company politics is basically a balance of power and relates to the struggle for power in the office. Picture a basketball game with your employees divided into two teams. Whoever has the ball in their court calls the shots. Office politics is just like that. It's about who's on whose side.

The major issue with company politics is that it does not benefit the business itself and doesn't contribute to its growth. For example, if you have a worker who is asking for a raise, this will add to your expenses. How does it help your business grow? After hearing that one employee is getting a raise, you may get more requests for raises from others. Once this situation occurs, company politics can get nasty.

As you cultivate your ideal business environment, keep company politics in mind and develop a business culture that minimizes office politics. Even if you decide to go with a culture that you believe is completely positive and free of company politics, it may turn out to be an instigator for potential negative issues that bring company politics along with them. Here are tips to help you minimize this type of conflict in your office:

1. Hire the right people. Remember that your employees will also be part of your business culture. You may have laid the foundation with core values, organizational systems, etc. but the key players are your team members. If they don't help to create and propagate the business culture you've envisioned, you'll have big obstacles ahead.

Get it right from the start by hiring the right people. Hire people who are ambitious and able to work toward your vision. Avoid adding team members who only think of their own gains. Hire candidates who are team players that value teamwork rather than people who don't want to get involved with others.

What you need here is good judgment. This doesn't mean you should base your decisions on your own assumptions. Someone who seems reserved may actually prove to be a great team member with leadership qualities just as someone who seems genuine and open may only be putting up a front. One way to help you judge others effectively is to hold a trial period with new or prospective employees to see how they fit in with your business culture.

If you end up hiring the wrong people, let go of them immediately to prevent any further issues. If potential problem employees stick around, you'll have a tougher time handling any challenges that may arise.

2. Prepare for any issues associated with company politics. Certain behaviors and activities can be catalysts for office politics, such as competition among employees, promotions and rewards. Let's take a common scenario that causes conflict as an example: when employees ask for a raise or promotion.

These encounters end up favoring the individual who's asking for a promotion instead of you, the CEO. If you're not careful about what you say, you may reveal too much of your own thoughts and feelings about the promotion. That's what gets the rumor mill going, which can turn employees against you. The best approach is to avoid saying much at all. Be vague, and mind your reactions – they can be used against you, too.

Consider the possible scenarios that may play out and develop a plan that you can execute if they become real-life situations. Evaluate your plans regularly and update them if you come up with new ideas for handling different problems.

3. Be objective. In some teams, certain employees may not work well together. If it gets bad enough, the involved parties may come to you to solve their issues. That can spell trouble for you. Depending on what actions you take, this can result in people in your business turning against you.

The people who are working for you will pay the greatest attention to what you do in these situations. If you fire one of the individuals involved in a conflict between coworkers, or if you show that you're biased toward or against a particular employee in any way, rumors can spread and people will start to lose respect for you.

It's crucial for you to avoid getting dragged into "he said, she said" situations and becoming the center of them. Sometimes it's better to encourage employees to work it out among themselves while you mediate. In that case, no one can blame you for anything.

You should also be careful about trying to defend certain employees and making it seem like the other party is to blame for the conflict. This can result in a rift between the workers in the office.

When it comes to employee-centered disputes, the most important tip is to quickly nip the conflict in the bud. Don't sweep problems under the rug. Instead, address them right away and then move on with your business. Think of these problems as something similar to high school scenes. What would you say or do as an authority figure who is giving advice to high school students? Remember: You're the leader, and you play fair. Be objective when it comes to these types of issues.

4. Let your employees do their own evaluations.

Managers or even the CEO, depending on the business, most often complete employee evaluations. Although regular employee evaluations are great and may serve as a great benefit to your business, they can cause conflicts in your office.

For instance, some employees may feel isolated, or some may see favoritism toward other team members. This can cause tension and divisions in the office. To prevent this from happening and to ultimately keep company politics out of the office, allow workers to complete their own evaluations. Let them track their progress toward business goals you've set for the team.

This method gives more responsibility to the employees. There's no room to direct anger or resentment toward you if employees and managers handle their own evaluations. Hold your employees accountable for their work. You'll also encourage more productivity by letting your team members evaluate themselves.

5. Maintain your CEO mindset. You're the CEO, and being the CEO means you know what you want in your business. If people try to push against your boundaries, stand firm. Always maintain your professional image – you don't want people to use your reactions against you.

Your CEO mindset can help you through sticky situations. Learn to be assertive and speak in a persuasive manner. Make sure everything you say makes sense, and have the facts ready to back up anything you say. Be logical and avoid getting into arguments that can be used against you.

Remind yourself that you're the CEO. Don't let anyone try to push the boundaries you've set up in your business, but also remember to be humble and sympathetic. Company politics is a game, and you're a fair player.

Office politics can affect your business negatively. Be prepared for the fact that you'll have to change the way you manage your business if you end up being a player in the company politics game. If it gets to that point, find solutions that will help you move forward with your business and squash the conflicts. It can get complicated, but you're the owner. Make sure you're doing things for yourself rather than trying to please others to avoid conflict. Face problems and overcome them with effective, positive strategies.

The Importance of Titles and Promotions

Since we just covered company politics and why they can be negative, you may be thinking, "Why bother with titles and promotions if they can cause company politics?" It's true that many businesses avoid using titles and promotions to keep a fair playing field and minimize company politics. Without titles and promotions, there wouldn't be any negative competition between employees. The CEO doesn't have to get caught in the middle of office politics. Eventually, many entrepreneurs realize they need to use job titles and an established promotions process to better organize and manage their businesses.

Let's go over job titles first. Why are they an important? One of the main reasons why your employees need job titles is for resume purposes. If employees decide to move on from your company and seek employment with another one, they need to know what position they held in your business. It may seem less professional or appropriate for them to describe their position as "the person you did this and that." Job titles are more professional, and most of the time they cut right to the chase. If someone tells you that he or she is a digital marketing specialist, you immediately understand his or her position or are at least able to get a general picture of what the individual does.

However, if you're firm about not using job titles in your business, you can at least tell employees how to respond to people when they're asked about their job position. You can tell them to say that the business they work for doesn't use job titles in order to create a sense of equality among the team. Instead of sharing their job position, they can mention describe their main responsibilities in the company.

Another reason why job titles are important to employees is because, at some point, your team members will need to know who does what. Job titles help employees to determine who to go to if they need help with an assignment. They also help your customers to know who to go to when they need assistance. For example, someone who does administrative tasks holds the title of personal assistant. This title indicates that this employee handles customer relations and lets customers know who to go to when they want to set up appointments with you.

Then there are promotions. Promotions can involve anything from raises to new job positions and titles. Unfortunately, promotions can become an area of conflict in the office. Let's say you have a web developer on your team who has been with you since the start of your business. You may promote the employee to a senior position, but other web developers on your team feel like you're showing favoritism toward this member of your business. This can cause other employees to think you promote people based on how many years they've been in your business instead of basing promotions on performance. One web developer may think he or she is much better at his or her job than the senior member and may feel undervalued as a result.

Promotions are beneficial for the employee. One of the biggest benefits that come with promotions is that employees can impress future employers. For example, if you promote someone to a higher job position, he or she can put that information on his or her resume. If the individual plans to work for another company in the future, the company will be impressed by the promotion.

Promotions can cause one of two things within a business: a team that is not united and works against itself, or a team that works together, congratulates each other for promotions, and supports each other. If you pick the right people for your business, promotions won't be the impetus for office politics. Instead, promotions will be welcomed and supported by the other team members.

To create an effective promotions process and job title management system, be transparent about everyone's positions, skills, and responsibilities. You can share this information with your team via an online portal or on another platform. You can also have meetings with your managers or other team members to discuss promotions. This makes your plans to promote a member of your team transparent, and will enable you to gain insight from other employees. Discussing promotions with others in this way can also help you to weed out any employees who may become problems in the future. Since these discussions require objective thinking, you can immediately spot other team members who are subjective in their judgment, i.e. those who pass around gossip about the person you're thinking of promoting. In these meetings you can learn more about your employees and spot any potential conflicts that may come up.

Keep in mind that every method is not bulletproof. Even if your processes are effective, it only takes one person who is against your chosen processes for promotions and job titles to cause trouble in your company. That's why it's crucial for you to be careful about who you hire. The people that you allow into your business are the ones who will carry the torch for you, or those who will prevent your business from moving forward.

When Smart People are Bad Employees

Having experienced and smart people on your team is like being served a gourmet meal on a silver platter. When you find out that gourmet meal was actually only takeout food from a cheap restaurant that was made to look gourmet, it's suddenly not as irresistibly appetizing.

Many companies focus on hiring employees from different backgrounds and developing a diverse team. In fact, having a team of people from different backgrounds can be incredibly valuable. A lot of companies also put emphasis on hiring intelligent, experienced employees. What most people don't realize is that smart employees can turn out to be bad ones, despite their talent. The most common issues are as follows:

1. The Ego

Some employees with lower job titles can be rude, unreasonable people. If these types of employees make it to higher positions that give them more power, their egos inflate. Even if the egotistical jerk is smart and does his or her job well, making the entire team feel uncomfortable isn't going to do any good for your long-term business goals.

The biggest problem that occurs when these types of employees are around is miscommunication. Let's say you have an egotistical employee as a manager for one of your departments. If the ego-driven manager makes it difficult for employees to communicate with him or her, how can that department move forward and work together to produce the results you want? If the egotistical manager wants it his or her way or the highway, how can other employees shine and provide great ideas, feedback, etc. to help boost your business?

Yes, the egotistical manager is an incredible employee with impressive skills and experience, but if he or she isn't helping your business to grow and isn't being a team player, it's time to let the person go. As they say, there are plenty of fish in the sea.

2. The Fault Finder

Constant improvements are an important part of the business growth process. If something doesn't work for your business, toss it aside and find a better solution. If an employee becomes an obstacle to reaching your business goals, it's time to let them go. After all, no business is perfect.

Despite knowing that a perfect business doesn't exist, what happens when you have a faultfinder on your team? Instead of working to help improve the company, all the person does is find fault and complain. Instead of focusing on improving his or her skills, they find fault with the company and let their opinions be known to others, influencing other employees' views and actions.

Even if the faultfinder performs well and gives you excellent results, this doesn't mean he or she is the best employee for your business. The faultfinder is motivated in countless ways, and these reasons vary depending on the person. Some possible reasons for their tendency to find fault include:

- Feeling like he or she doesn't have enough power or control in the business, leading them to complain about the company.
- Complaining and finding faults in the business to hide his or her own insecurities.
- Having the need to rebel.
- Misunderstanding the company, his or her responsibilities, etc. and not wanting others to find out, so complaining is the only way to hide this.

When you have a faultfinder on your team, pay attention to any signs that may indicate a potential propensity for future problems. If you hear that this employee frequently complains about you or any part of your business yet you don't take action, the situation can escalate quickly. In this situation the faultfinder has often already built a team of followers, which helps to build his or her credibility and makes you look like the losing team. However, this doesn't mean you have to feel like you're being backed into a corner. If faultfinders come to you with complaints about the company, turn the situation around on them and kill them with kindness. Thank them for their feedback and let them know that you'll look into the problem areas and see what you can do.

This method works especially well against weak-willed faultfinders because they will see that you can roll with the punches and they fail to do any damage to you. At this point, the faultfinders will get bored and move on to something else. Execute this tactic from the beginning. Otherwise the faultfinders will already feel empowered by their complaints and the presence of their team of followers, and they will not be influenced by your behavior.

If you let the faultfinder stay in your company for too long, morale among your team members can shift and go downhill fast. If killing faultfinders with kindness doesn't work right away, it's time for you to fire them. Take a Donald Trump-esque zero-tolerance attitude toward anyone who doesn't value the morale of your company.

Even if the employee is brilliant at what he or she does, if your company's culture is at stake you should fire the person right away. If anyone else doesn't agree with you and your decision to fire that employee, you can let them go as well.

3. The Missing Person

Picture this scenario: You hire a stellar employee who does flawless work and completes assignments days or even weeks before deadlines arrive. Suddenly, the incredible employee that you hired disappears. He doesn't call in when he misses days of work. He comes in late when he does decide to show up. He turns in low-quality work. And you're stuck wondering what the heck happened.

Despite being an excellent team member, the employee who becomes a missing person isn't reliable. Your entire team and business can't function properly or move forward with a flake in the group. In the case of dealing with a missing person, you have to let the person go. Even if it pains you to fire someone who is talented, you're the CEO and you must keep the bigger picture in mind. If you can't rely on one employee, your entire team will fall apart. Your entire business will fall soon after, if you let the situation get to that point.

When you're faced with one or more of these types of employees, consider it a test of your own values and goals for your business. Even if an employee makes huge, positive contributions to your business, if they don't contribute anything to your business culture, which do you value more? It's your job as the CEO to make these big decisions for your company. Each decision you make will impact your business, so make the right ones. Set boundaries, and get rid of anything or anyone who crosses those boundaries.

How to Create Core Values for Your Company and Live by Them

Core values are the backbone of your business. These core values will guide you to the right paths for your business. With every decision you're faced with, your core values will show you the right way. These values will also help you to build the ideal business culture for your company.

Not only does your business benefit from having core values, but the people you work with, including customers and suppliers, can benefit from your core values as well. Countless companies associate their values with profits, which is commonly known as ROV or return on values.

Think about it this way: When customers buy a product from you or invest in a service from your business, they're also purchasing your brand and working with a business that has the same values as they do. That's why setting up values for your company forms a stronger, more successful business foundation.

Let's break down the process of how to create core values for your company, and how you and your team can stick with them:

1. Brainstorm. Make a list of basic core values that you want for your business. These can include things like integrity, strong communication, leadership, teamwork, and excellent customer service. Think about the vision you have for your company. What values do you need to support your vision? Consider your ideal business culture as well – this can help you to determine the basic core values that you want for your business.

Also focus on values that you believe in. Avoid emphasizing values that you *aspire* to have – you may end up neglecting to follow these values later on, which can damage your credibility with your employees, work partners and clients. You can evaluate your own personal values and employ them as your company's core values to start with.

2. Be specific. Make your core values detailed and specific. Use them as part of your work processes. Don't just let them sit on a shelf and gather dust. Make them actionable and commit yourself to utilizing them.

For example, let's say one of your main core values is strong communication. Take this one step further: Consider how you can create open, strong communication within your team and with other people that you do business with. You know the *what* (strong communication) so now it's time to figure out the *how*. Ask yourself this question with every core value you set up: How can you incorporate your values into your everyday business life?

It is also important to hold your employees accountable for following the core values of your business. Make it clear that you're serious about following the core values and hire and fire accordingly. Show people that your core values aren't just pretty words that you generated to impress others. Rather, you live by them and so do your employees.

3. Make your core values interesting and fun. "We value our customers." What does this statement sound like to you? Dry, dull and general, right? Make your company stand out by turning the expression of your core values into something that's interesting to read. Get people excited to learn more about your company based on these core values. Don't use generic, boring statements. Talk to your team to help you come up with interesting core value statements that represent your brand.

4. Remind your team of the company's core values frequently. From meetings to employee evaluations, remind your team of your company's core values on a regular basis. Not only does this help enforce your values and show that you're committed to them, it also helps to reinforce these values and to teach employees to internalize and live by them.

Train your employees to think according to these values when they work on projects or interact with clients. Make sure everyone on your team is on the same page and continues to live by your core values as long as they're a part of your company. Remember that you're the leader, and you also need to live by the values you set for your company. Be an example for your employees.

5. Adjust your core values when necessary. As the business owner, you must be willing to make changes. If situations come up that go against your core values, it may be time to reevaluate and upgrade them.

This doesn't mean you have to change them constantly to accommodate any conflicts that may arise. When you're faced with a big obstacle that tests you and your business values, that's when you should review them and see if it's time to make changes. Don't be afraid to make changes to your values when this becomes essential to the growth of your business.

When you feel it's time to adjust your core values, talk to your team members and discuss the changes that you're planning to make with them. Get feedback from your team, and brainstorm with them to come up with the best approach to implementing these changes. By allowing your team members to be part of the process and being open to their ideas, you'll build better relationships with them. This is also a great opportunity to improve teamwork, especially if teamwork is part of your company's core values.

Have fun creating your core values. You're creating the foundation of your business, so don't make it a chore for yourself. If you have a tough time formulating your core values, utilize basic ones for now and add to your list as the business grows.

In our next book, the journey continues. Learn about effective leadership, smart money management, and why learning to develop an intelligent team is important to becoming a successful entrepreneur.